MIA SANCHEZ

Symphony of Secrets

A Poetry Collection

Copyright © 2022 by Mia Sanchez

All rights reserved. No part of this publication may be reproduced, stored or transmitted in any form or by any means, electronic, mechanical, photocopying, recording, scanning, or otherwise without written permission from the publisher. It is illegal to copy this book, post it to a website, or distribute it by any other means without permission.

Mia Sanchez asserts the moral right to be identified as the author of this work.

First edition

This book was professionally typeset on Reedsy. Find out more at reedsy.com

This poetry collection is a dedication to those who have always encouraged me to follow my passion. I appreciate you always having my back and allowing me to create this book.

Contents

Preface		iii
1	The Other Side	1
2	Empty Promises	3
3	The Blame Game	5
4	Misfit	7
5	Misunderstood Me	8
6	Introvert's View	10
7	The Most Perfect Life	12
8	The Silent Fight	14
9	The Worst Place	16
10	Fever Dream	18
11	A Year of Regrets	20
12	Hidden Shadows	22
13	Empty Conversation	24
14	After Us	26
15	The Horrible Wait	28
16	Online	30
17	The In-Between	32
18	Miles Away	34
19	Never Coming Back	36
20	Overrated Apologies	38
21	The Suicide Note	40
22	Ten Years Later	42
23	It's Been A Little While	44

24	The Changes	47
25	Midnight Scars	49
26	Empty Promises	51
27	Tuesday Evening	53
28	Another Hello	55
29	Sometimes	57
30	Looking At Your Eyes	59
31	Beautiful Tomorrow	61
32	I Won't Give This Up	63
33	It's Okay	65
34	Fragile	67
35	Our Safe Space	69
About the Author		71

Preface

Like most people in the world, I grew up as a teenager who believed no one understood her. Now as a software developer, I have finally found the courage to dive deep into the world of words and find ways to express myself as I have never done before.

My poems in this book are quite literally the most honest, I have ever been. I have written about the things that mattered to me and the people I always wished I had said something to at least once.

These poems are based on random topics I picked out myself and then decided to write about them based on what I have experienced.

I was surprised when I realized that I managed to write poems that told a specific story even though I was writing about random topics. I hope readers can follow the storyline and enjoy it as well. I absolutely adored writing these poems and I hope you can enjoy reading them!

I hope you can relate to at least some of these and be happy that you are not the only ones feeling such emotions in this crazy world.

1

The Other Side

The distance between us cannot be cleared:
You have never tried to come to the other side.
Will you ever dare and care to know my perspective?
Or will you always think you have endured the most?

Your happiness is all you have ever cared about;
Mine is left in the dust of your countless mistakes.
Yet, I never found the strength to blame you for it.
How could I despise the one I was born to love?

I have stayed an entire lifetime on the other side:
Yearning, that, one day, you will hear my explanation.
But you have always chosen your false truths;
Calling me an enemy when I only wanted your love.

I remember: thinking you must be heartbroken;
Too tired to realize I haven't done anything wrong,

Always hoping that somehow I could help you be happy.
But you close the door; shutting it whenever I try to enter

So, I always remained on the other side.
The world stripped me bare of anything I ever felt.
Weak as I was, I couldn't clarify anything to you then;
That's how you found another reason to hate me now.

I gave you the confidence to believe I will always wait;
No matter how you hurt me, I was there for you again.
Using me up till the very last piece of me faded away;
Then, you ran through the vacant room, trying to find me.

It might seem difficult, but all you need to do is be here;
Holding on to my hand tight as I introduce you to my world.
But I knew dreaming for you to love me back was too much:
For, Your insecurities always kept you on the other side.

2

Empty Promises

I remember that day as if it happened yesterday.
You looked into my eyes and sounded so genuine;
I believed when you promised to try a little more;
To learn my point of view like you never did before.

A moment earlier, I had decided to let you go finally
Whispering goodbye like I should have done years ago.
But your grin blinded my sight like any other evening;
I smiled back, ready to try a little more for you again.

Any motive I had, froze on my tongue as you talked.
You gave me hope that we might have a nice future:
Promise after promise; saying every word I desired.
Just like that, you won the war for the millionth time.

Shattered hard, yet I loved you throughout;
Recalling your words each time I wanted to give up;
I gave away secrets and weaknesses, Trusting you;
hoping you would stay beside me and be in love.

Lately, I have been walking through our house alone.
Your empty promises lay there like my broken heart.
Now scars run deep in my soul as I continue to live,
Trying to make peace with the memories you left behind.

Perhaps you knew that forever was a distant dream;
Something you suspected we would never get to see.
But you gave me rationales to believe it was a thing.
Now, you converse as if it was nothing but agony.

It's been years since the night you walked away.
It took me months, but I concluded you had moved on.
But memories still cloud my eyes on some rainy days.
Then, again, I start to believe your empty promises.

3

The Blame Game

The blame game you have played-
Has it given you any satisfaction?
Does it make you happy to hurt me;
Treating me this badly when I did nothing?

Do you think it makes it easier?
To accuse me of things I never even did?
Does it lessen the hurt you are feeling?
Or are you setting up for future remorse?

How did you forget so easily what I did;
When I stayed by your side on hard days?
Do you still remember those harsh nights when,
Despite being hurt, I stayed to ensure you are okay.

I know that you have been through plenty;
That a part of you doesn't want this pain;
But do you think this is all just my mistake
When I am hurt almost as much as you are?

We could have talked and found a remedy.
But you just elected to take it all out on me,
Leaving me silent because of your words.
Things you said injured me; I hope you know.

I hope you know I could accuse you too;
Say that I've suffered a lot because of you.
But I held myself back so you don't get hurt.
But in return, you gave me poisonous words.

You will come tomorrow asking for my help,
You will be mad that I have nothing left to say.
But isn't it you to be blamed for being silent?
Would you still remember this time that day?

I sat down with tears pouring down my face.
I thought I was the worst person for hurting you.
When I know, this isn't my fault in any way;
I was doing my work to make things easier.

But here I am, trapped in your blame game.
Would it be wrong for me to offer you hate?
That's all I've ever gotten from you anyway.
Why is it bad if I give you back the same now?

4

Misfit

She has never been that kind:
A person who fits into a group;
Both physically and mentally;
She has always been the different one.

She never had normal hobbies;
Never did anything in a normal way.
Her mind had the weirdest thoughts;
And dreams that seemed impossible.

Often, she was looked down on
Just because she was a little unusual.
Yet, she put on a beautiful smile
And tried hard to mix in with the crowd.

They never realized her potential:
For, she was made to be different.
To not be tied with painful chains:
But to fly higher than anyone else.

5

Misunderstood Me

Will you ever understand how it feels:
To be mistaken when you say nothing?
She lives a more varied life than what you see;
But you don't think it's crucial to know her.

She gets ignored by the ones she adores;
She always gets missed in crowds; no one cares.
She never gets to express her opinions out loud;
Her words always sound naive to people.

She believed in weirder things than the rest;
She loved you as no one else had ever done;
She gave you company when you needed it;
She spent time with you when you were sad.

You stared at her and thought she didn't care;
The stoic look on her face never changed.
You failed to see the misery behind her smile;
So, you asserted she was nothing but violent.

Now she has lost interest in helping you to know her.
She is too tired to make you believe in her again.
You can continue to misunderstand her now.
But was it really fair to never have given her a chance?

You might think you know exactly who she is
But she was only misinterpreted every time
She wonders how it feels not to be called a culprit;
Would she be able to feel that emotion someday?

She wanted to write about the "misunderstood her":
Maybe now you know how it feels to be like her.
Will you ever think twice before you blame her?
Perhaps you will continue to assert that she is selfish.

6

Introvert's View

You might recall that one person in the room,
Sitting in the very back and talking to no one:
The one that was known as the introverted kind-
The title that they heard more than their name.

I am one of those, so maybe I could help you
Understand the world from an introvert's view.
Do you ever wonder what makes them so silent?
When the world gives us reasons to complain,

Introverts have loud thoughts they can't ignore.
They think twice before doing one single thing;
Scared of making mistakes and gaining attention;
Be judged by people they want some love from.

Carry heavy secrets in their chest as they live,
But they struggle to talk to random strangers.
Introverts aren't rude but too anxious to speak.
That's why they always get left behind alone.

INTROVERT'S VIEW

Deep conversations make them the happiest
Debates are what they want to avoid the most;
They choose to hear what the world has to say;
But the world never bothers to hear them.

They desire their space more than the others;
When the world drains them a little too much,
They hope for someone to stay beside them;
Loving uneasy silences yet precious moments.

Introverts might seem strange and rude to you;
But they are simply striving to be comfortable;
Discover people that spend time to know them;
Someone who loves them without any judgment.

7

The Most Perfect Life

It's so simple to dismiss this reality;
Pretend everything in life is amazing;
Put a happy smile on my face again,
And resume surviving a noisy life.

So loud inside my head right now;
Though I am voiceless on the outside,
Trying to make sense of these things,
Trying to learn what I could get done.

I fail to pull myself away from my bed,
I can't fix myself so I can face the world;
Confirming that my eyes don't show signs
Of the restless nights, I have had so far.

Pleasant in front of practical strangers;
Cheerful in front of those I called family;
Trapped behind the eyes that shine well:
My heart has many problems to discuss.

THE MOST PERFECT LIFE

Exhausted to the point, I struggle to stand;
Yet, my feet refused to give up beneath me;
I wish it was easy to forget all the hurt ;
I wish it was that easy for me to move on.

My pride always came in between though,
Making it difficult for me to ask for help.
So, I resumed fighting all my wars alone;
Even when I knew I wouldn't be able to win.

I wish I wasn't good at the pretense game.
Then maybe I would see a different life;
An edition that others saw but not me.
And told me I had the most perfect life.

8

The Silent Fight

She wanted to talk for hours that night.
But somehow, she didn't find any word
To express the constant pain in her chest.
So, She kept quiet and ignored it completely.

Each day she swerved back into the silence.
The more people refused to understand her
The more it made her want to yell at them
But she couldn't find the vigor to speak more.

There was a time when she talked for days;
Never struggling to form perfect sentences;
Now her head was too much of a mess;
She could only write words on clear paper.

She saw pain flooding those beautiful eyes;
She tried to reach out but fell short at that time.
They stayed, but she turned more into silence;
The ones she loved were destroyed in the end.

THE SILENT FIGHT

What the hell was wrong with her recently?
Why was she terrible at finding her powers?
How could she face the ones she loved,
Now that she had changed a lot once more?

She used to cheer them and do a lot more,
she tried lesser than she used to;
She yearned to figure out all the reasons;
She wanted to fix things more than others.

For once, she hoped she could talk to them;
That she could tell them that she was okay;
She was trying to find her voice back again.
Finally, she would become as they knew her.

9

The Worst Place

Stuck inside my mind for weeks now:
I want to know how to get out of here.
I wish I could tell you what was wrong;
But no longer can I find the right words.

The worst place to be is in here for sure;
Nowhere else do I suffocate this much.
You want me to tell you why I was hiding?
I hope you know that this isn't my choice.

I walk through the routine without issues;
People see me and say I am doing okay.
They say I am happy after breaking them;
But they don't see the wounds on my soul.

Someone like me would always be alone;
Struggling to speak even with million words
You might think it's easier to be on my own;
But I would rather be anywhere but here.

THE WORST PLACE

This place has held me captive for many years;
Making me think I can't do anything well.
Even when I have everything like others have,
I always believe that I am the most pathetic.

I write on paper because I can't explain well;
They say I have issues that can't be fixed.
I want to say one day; things will be better;
But I can't have hope in this stark darkness.

The worst place to be for me is right here:
Stuck inside my head; feeling more helpless.
I hope one day someone will come to find
The girl that only wants to escape this hell.

10

Fever Dream

Do you also wake up in the middle of each night;
Wanting to believe that it was only a fever dream?
Sweat runs down your back as you try to fall asleep,
But the scene in front of your eyes keeps you awake.

As if it was just yesterday when you were happy;
Talking about a future that seemed easy to have;
Love in your eyes for those you wanted forever;
And You ask yourself if it was nothing but a dream

Now you wake up in the future you wanted then;
Different than what you once thought it would be.
You smile yet the pain continues to grow in you;
You think about things you can do to repair this:

Messed up as it is now it is just like a dream.
You ask yourself if it ever was a reality you had.
But, then all the memories run down your cheeks;
And you realize maybe it was reality a while ago:

FEVER DREAM

A fever dream is all you call it when people ask.
A reality that now appears to never come back.
You are not sure if you even want to live it again;
But a part of you still wants to experience it again.

What is it really, a fever dream or a nightmare?
You don't know but still want to live through it;
Silence so loud you can't avoid your thoughts;
You can no longer say it was just a fever dream.

11

A Year of Regrets

Never have I found the accurate words
To narrate the year that transformed me.
But, if I had to select one from the long list,
"Regrets" will depict that year quite perfectly.

It was the year when I loved many people;
Back then, it felt like something so wrong.
The most incredible feeling I ignored then,
Now is remorse that I carry along with me.

I got into a pattern where I never got sleep;
Worked hard yet never felt content or happy.
I tried not to think about those who left me;
Yet, I replaced them with other similar faces.

Tiny minutes of peace that ended instantly;
I craved answers but collected more issues:
The grief that took over me without a reason;
Pleasure seemed a little further away every day.

A YEAR OF REGRETS

It was a year when I lost and found so much.
I made many memories, but cannot recall them;
Many relationships that I ruined due to sorrow;
I met new people, but I didn't even talk to them.

A year, when, without you, I resumed living life;
Saying I didn't miss you, yet cried every night.
I took writing seriously because I couldn't talk;
I began new stories but never ended even one.

Many regrets I can recollect from that year;
I made a hundred errors as I struggled to live.
Love beside me, but I couldn't clutch onto it;
I think about those days and count my regrets.

12

Hidden Shadows

She buried their love in her chest;
Like a secret never to be exposed.
She always walked past him easily;
As if her heart didn't belong to him.

The world believed she was lonely:
She wasn't known to love anything.
Behind the doors, she wrote for him
Many letters that he never even saw.

She tried hard to forget he existed;
She wished his smile wasn't pretty;
She craved to keep him beside her.
But the one he loved was never her.

So, she put a fake smile on her face.
She gave him everything he needed;
She never wished he would love her;
But her heart wasn't simple to satisfy.

HIDDEN SHADOWS

He has moved away from their love.
Now he walks down the street alone;
Wishing for someone who isn't his.
But she continues to love him some more

Once upon a time, he wanted her too;
But she was too scared to accept him.
Now, he no longer remembers her grin;
But she only recalls his smile the most.

Her emotions are like hidden shadows,
Unknown to him, but they are still here.
Every night, she dreams about that time,
She then jots down a few more poems.

13

Empty Conversation

A part of me is always frightened ;
Thinking one day, we may not speak.
How am I supposed just to move on
When you will leave me with so many things?

Days when I decline to talk to anyone,
Knowing your patience also runs out a lot.
I wish one day you won't just give up
Even when say you will try for me again.

I don't know what's wrong with me lately;
Too depleted to figure out my emotions;
I just yearn for the night to come sooner,
So, I can close my eyes and fall asleep.

Back to having the same song on repeat;
Words that don't have any impact on me;
My mind is plagued with so many thoughts;
Yet, I am unable to focus on any one of them.

EMPTY CONVERSATION

My fingers hover over my keyboard again;
I type something and then delete it later;
I think it all sounds foolish and vacant:
I allow the silence to fill the empty gaps.

I think about you each second of the day:
My heart knows you have waited for me as well.
But my head can't come up with words
As I sag against the couch, tired at night.

I hope you can give me a bit more time,
I drag myself to become better for you;
But somehow, the discussion stays vacant;
I resume filling these notepad pages again.

14

After Us

I struggle to smile recklessly tonight;
I can't keep up with the discussion.
I still pretend well that I am happy,
But the space beside me stays empty.

I am reminded of the day that we last talked;
You were also at a loss for words that night.
I was helpless since I couldn't say anything;
I watched you drifting further away every second.

We were perfect, but it was never enough:
We continued to make the same mistakes;
Similar problems continued to damage us;
I stayed away from you out of all the guilt.

Tonight is just the result of that evening:
I am around strangers that don't even care.
In the end, they will return to their loved ones
And, I will continue to search for you in the room.

AFTER US

I know that you are never coming back again;
But I wish we would both be better soon.
I suffocate as I struggle to breathe deeper;
Once again, I am waiting for you to find me.

We promised each other forever back then;
Now your eyes don't even recognize mine.
I used to believe you would always love me;
But now you cannot even say words to me.

You told me it would be easier if we walked out;
I am not yet ready to see the end of us: not just yet.
Maybe I can assure you one last time to learn
That the life after us is not what I need at all.

15

The Horrible Wait

You struggled so much to talk to me:
You would rather watch me in secret.
I continued to crumble in front of you;
Yet, you continued to pretend I was okay.

What was so terrible about my words?
You found it simpler to hide from me
My eyes were stuck to the screen for days;
I wished you would just reply to me once.

Each time that I waited for you to text,
A part of me evaporated into the thin air;
My broken heart was often too hard to fix;
My eyes were too exhausted to stay open.

Your absence always broke me completely:
Making it difficult for me even to breathe.
How could I even suffer so much
Even when I knew you needed space badly?

THE HORRIBLE WAIT

It was always impossible for me to speak;
How much I was ready to do for your smile;
I wanted you but was too scared to confess;
Maybe thus, you never knew my true feelings.

I knew that you knew where you could find me
You knew I had been waiting there for hours;
Still hoping you would come to see me once
And just to make sure I am doing alright

Forgive me cause I gave up too quickly at times;
I had always tried my very best to adore you.
My love, that might seem too dramatic at times
Even though I never wanted to burden you

Endless mistakes that I know I also made
But I don't ever regret falling in love with you.
I tried beyond my capacities and my strength;
I just wanted to find more ways to keep you here.

16

Online

I know you check when was the last time I was online;
Have a ton to say yet you never let go of your silence.
Then you complain I never come and talk to you here;
Complaining that I am too selfish to come online tonight.

You think that I don't see the damage we have caused;
You think I am good at ignoring whatever you do
Too busy in your head, you never see all my struggles
Then you ask me why I never open my mouth to speak.

"Us" not being online- do you think that's the issue?
As if when we are, you always have so much to tell me.
I would rather be offline than wait for you to write back:
The anxiety it gives me has become too much to handle.

You need to learn to judge yourself before you hurt me:
Saying words you never mean just cause you are angry.
You are gonna regret them later then you will apologize:
You need to know that your "sorry" doesn't erase the hurt.

ONLINE

Know that I wait for you to come online just like you do
What will it take for us to realize the worth of all of this?
I don't give you my time, but no one else gets it too!
I have been lonelier yet you don't see all of these issues!

I have been beside you for more time than I can count
Yet, you think I forgot you just because I am never online?
I don't need to be online to think about you all the time
But you don't see it as you are too blinded by your anger.

Hope one day my online status doesn't matter as much;
That our friendship isn't hurt by my absence on the net.
But for now, I don't have any other way to convince you
What can I do if you can never see past my online status?

17

The In-Between

It's been many days since we both went our separate ways.
I should have moved on by now, but it's not that simple;
For, the in-between has been caging me here for all this time.
I have tried to move on, but your memories won't let me.

Sometimes I look at my phone and wish you would text;
I smile to myself, knowing well that what we had is gone
Yet, I continue to look at the pictures we once took here;
We seemed so happy back then, people mistook it for love.

Nowadays, it's hard to know what we had all those years
You shattered my heart, but only after I broke yours:
Fights that lingered longer than moments of happiness;
Yet, we assured each other to try to be forever together.

Now the in-between is filled with all of my regrets:
Lately, I spend hours trying to recall where it all went wrong.
Maybe it was a slow change we were too busy to notice;
Or perhaps we saw and chose to look past it conveniently.

THE IN-BETWEEN

A part of me is frantic to give you the chance you want;
Another part is terrified that history will only repeat itself.
We were so convinced it was the right time to move on
Yet, I look for your texts still, and you wait for me to return.

The fear of the unseen hurts us, but we continue;
We're both hurt, yet we don't know how to close the gaps.
I thought we were both so sure about everything each time.
Yet here we are, unable to break away from the in-between.

18

Miles Away

It's been the toughest night ever
To stay without you by my side
I am trying my best to reach you
But you seem miles away already

A faint sound of your sweet voice
Echoes in this blurred mind of mine
It's hard to recognize everything now
But I can still pick out your laughter

You haven't said anything in a while
Yet I can still hear the constant blame
You have sealed your heart shut now
But I can still see the hurt seeping out

I am trying not to break down tonight
Without you, I am trying to survive here
I try to find one reason to stay alive
But I can only see the tears in your eyes

MILES AWAY

If I had known it was the last goodbye
I would have been careful with my words
I want to go and take everything back
But I can feel it's too late for that now

Now I watch the lonely moon in the sky
Tell him the story of how I lost my love
I decided to replace you with the moon
But he is never going to be as good as you

19

Never Coming Back

I turned on the front porch lights tonight
Around the time when you should be home
But then at midnight, I turned them off again
Knowing that you wouldn't come back home

I played your favorite tunes on the old piano
I sang mindlessly the song you loved the most
I wished for you to walk in and sing with me
Then I realized your favorite song has changed

I sat on the balcony to watch the sunset alone
I waited for you to come and watch it with me
But when the sun was long gone I went inside
I convinced myself that you didn't care anymore

I came back home and walked into the kitchen
Pictured you cooking food with a beautiful smile
But then I settled on the chair with a wine bottle

NEVER COMING BACK

I finally knew you were never coming home now

I lit up your favorite candle inside our bedroom
I lay on the bed hoping to picture you beside me
But our last argument was all I could remember
Then I knew it was my fault you were not in there

That was the moment I finally realized the reality
That you were too far gone to return back home
Now it was time for me to move past all the pain
It was time for me to leave your memories behind

Tears ran down my cheeks, yet I smiled as I cleaned
As I took down our photos from the walls that night
I recalled the good times and blamed myself more
At that moment, I finally allowed myself to mourn

Maybe I loved you more than you could love me
Maybe you loved me too much to be hurt by me
I gave you my baggage but refused to take yours
And maybe that's why you'll never come back now

20

Overrated Apologies

I know you will make the same mistakes:
Once and maybe a few more times again.
I'll accept your apologies every single time
It makes me think, are you a fool, or is it me?

People say all of us must get another chance;
For, We treat others bitterly only when we are hurt.
It's okay to forgive as long as they come back.
But how can a simple sorry fix all that's broken?

How can I know if you didn't mean any harm?
You say you did it due to a temporary weakness
Unintentionally maybe, but you still destroyed me
Now you want to come back to ask for forgiveness.

You miss me when you remember how I saved you:
I have lent you everything you have ever needed.
You see how I was there even when you were silent-
That's when you realize you've never treated me well.

OVERRATED APOLOGIES

That's why you always come with new apologies;
I hear your explanations, but you never hear mine.
I say it's okay and take you back to hurt me more
Even when I know the same thing will happen again.

A circle of despair that I cannot escape from now;
The word "sorry" is thus the one I despise the most.
I can forgive you, but I can't forget what you did:
I'm afraid I'm too exhausted to give you any more.

I don't want to ignore your mistakes anymore;
I won't say it's okay just because I feel bad for you;
No longer is it alright for you to hurt me some more;
So, now I won't take any of your overrated apologies!

21

The Suicide Note

A suicide note that I have written:
As I kill whatever is between us
Left broken in numerous pieces
On the cold ground beneath us.

Hidden behind the empty stare
Apologies that I have never said
Too hurt to care about your pain;
Too tired to give a damn about us.

Scribbled in an unknown language
Words that I have hardly jotted down
Describing the situation that I am in
But, it's something you won't ever see.

I am exhausted beyond belief now;
Too fragile to battle against myself.
Ready to approve the final goodbye;
Settled sweetly on your elegant lips.

THE SUICIDE NOTE

The end that dances across my eyes;
I try to avoid it as much as I can
But the desire to sit silently won over;
My heart that wants to hold you near

Apologies seem unfair after crimes
That you have committed without knowing
Because my heart is still shattered
By the one who was supposed to stay

So this note is all I can compose tonight
The night ends with another heartbreak
Offering me just numbness gifted by you;
Stillbesides me when you aren't really here.

22

Ten Years Later

I closed my eyes, too tired to say things
I opened them, and you had gone away
Ten years have already passed by now
We aren't like how we once used to be.

Somehow all bridges have burned completely;
Miles away from you, I continue to live.
A part of me wishes to have you back;
A part of me knows its not worth it now.

From the playground where we played
To this bedroom, I have come a long way.
But I know I can still close my eyes shut
And picture you beside me just as quickly.

I heard you have a stable job now; at least
I work twenty hours more than I used to.
Some days I wish to tell you I am ruined,
But mostly, I know you still mean too much.

TEN YEARS LATER

It's been years since I walked away from you:
I remember the day when I said I hated you;
Numerous nights have passed since then:
I try to convince myself that's still the truth.

Hung up on cocaine, you texted me gibberish;
The following day I woke up to an empty screen.
It's almost as if I made up those scenarios:
Just to forget the perfect past behind me.

There are days when I cry myself to sleep;
Scrolling through the texts I sent you before
I see our mistakes; midst waves of laughter;
I wish we could have fixed things back then.

I guess life is better than it has been before;
Better than what killed us all those years;
I am breathing better with less heartache.
Still, sometimes I struggle to move forward.

I want to close my eyes, but I can't anymore.
Out of that bubble, a weird reality I can see.
What I should have always paid attention to;
But loving you was always far easier than it.

23

It's Been A Little While

It's been a little while.
A while since that night
When I was the happiest
Smiling right back at you.

It's been a little while
Since I saw happiness.
Things used to be better;
It is now a daily struggle.

It's been a little while
Since I wasn't all alone.
Friends are non-existent;
As if I never had them ever.

It's been a little while
Since I was madly in love.
With life or with someone;
As if it had never happened.

IT'S BEEN A LITTLE WHILE

It's been a little while
Since you have seen me smile.
Now I am just jealous of those
who moved on a long time ago.

It's been a little while
Since I've been comfortable.
Strangers offer me love now;
Yet I can't seem to accept it.

It's been a little while
Since I saw those I love.
Missing them every night;
Yet can't seem to find them.

It's been a little while
I hope things change soon.
Wanting to let go of all sorrows;
Wanting to fall in love once more.

It's been a little while:
But I know it's all on me.
I was the one to walk away;
So, now I have to walk alone.

It's been a little while:
Forgive me for missing out;
My broken heart is terrified;
Yet, it wishes to seek out love.

It's been a little while

Since you heard my secrets.
Sadness mustn't hide your grins;
So, I smile right back some more.

24

The Changes

A new morning comes with new changes:
People came and went but I am still here;
Waiting for the impossible to come true:
I still continue to fight every single hour.

I have some new issues as well now:
Few new things that hurt me more lately.
Still, I stand tall for those I love so much;
Hoping to be new like all the new changes.

So each day, I take it one second at a time:
Fighting each moment so the next is better.
No luck most times but I still keep hoping;
Maybe one day the change will be easy.

The changes are visible in the mirror at times;
But most days I feel like I am still the same.
But some nights I also see the helplessness:
Those nights I refuse to accept the changes.

Some changes make me guilty for being me:
For never changing the world wanted me to.
Those are the day when I struggle to keep up;
I fear that maybe I will get left behind soon.

Some changes are easy, while others aren't:
People ensure me time will amend this pain.
Smile in response is all I manage to do now,
Wanting to believe one day this will be okay.

For me, changes have never been simple;
I have always been the one to love routines.
But now I know changes are bound to come,
So, now I try to smile and get ready for them.

Every new day will bring a few new changes;
What else can I do but learn to accept them?
Hope one day they won't make me fade away;
I will keep fighting till I beat the new changes.

25

Midnight Scars

We talked at midnight most of the time
The rest of the day, we never got to talk
Several duties that we had to complete
Made it impossible to send a single text.

The moon was our spectator all those nights
Under the night sky, we shared our secrets.
Tears and chuckles that we both exchanged,
As we talked about a million random things.

Lovely memories that are inked on my skin:
Like midnight scars that will never vanish.
No matter how hard I try to get rid of you,
Your smile now invades all my lonely nights.

Things that I used to tell only you back then;
My diary is the one that discovers them lately.
I write rhymes to find a distraction for a while
But it doesn't allow me to miss you any less.

Do you yearn to call me to talk at midnight?
Do you have midnight scars on your heart?
Maybe you already found my replacements:
Now your nights are spent in their company.

I wish I hadn't added you to my routine then;
Now without you, I struggle to stay happy.
The moon abandoned me the day you left;
The midnight isn't as amazing to me anymore.

I hope all these scars fade away with time:
One day I won't remember you at midnight.
I will replace your memories with my own;
I will make the midnight mine and not ours.

26

Empty Promises

I remember the day clearly still today
You looked sincere when you talked
I believed when you said you'll try more
To learn things from my point of view.

A moment before I tried to let you go
I should have said goodbye days ago
But your smile blinded me once more
I smiled and said I would try a little more.

All reasons froze on my tongue then
You promised me a nice future again
Back then, you offered me happiness
And that's how you took over my life.

Broken heart, but I continued to love
Your promises never let me give up
I gave you every secret I had hidden
In return, I hoped you would love me.

But lately, I walk past empty hallways
Your empty promises lay on the floor
Scars on my heart, but I still try to live;
Try to walk past all memories you left.

Maybe you knew forever wasn't ours;
Maybe you knew we wouldn't see it.
But you did make me believe forever;
Now you talk as if we meant nothing.

Years passed since you walked away;
It took me months to move on too.
Memories cloud my eyes sometimes
Then, I remember your empty promises.

27

Tuesday Evening

We conversed for hours that Tuesday evening:
You blabbered about things that I didn't know.
I continued to stare at you with a small smile;
Hoping that you won't see that I needed you.

Back then, I knew you could break my heart;
I had been loved wrong in the past by others.
Your smile reminded me of those memories;
But I still hoped for you not to be like them.

I was naive and struggled to express things:
I never told you just how much I loved you.
Each morning I prayed for you to stay here;
But knew one day you would leave for sure.

You brought along the best time of my life;
Giving me reasons to love myself more.
I thought I never wanted to find love again;
But I still wished for you to love me back.

I loved you, so I believed the fake reality;
I trusted you when you promised to stay;
I told you I was ready to try hard for you;
With you by my side, I was happy to be alive.

People say I will be in love again one day
But maybe you were the right one for me.
Our timing never was perfect; I am aware.
But the memories you left are still perfect.

Tonight is another Tuesday evening finally;
I smile as I see your new social media posts;
You seem to have found someone new to love;
I chuckle because I know I still only love you.

I used to hate Tuesday evenings after you left:
All they reminded me of were your pretty smiles.
But now those memories keep me company too,
So, I eagerly wait for every new Tuesday evening.

28

Another Hello

She saw him and wanted to say hello.
Then, she hesitated and walked away.
He never knew that she was around;
The one before him was on her mind.

She remembered the last heartbreak
And recalled the first innocent "hello".
She recalled the first night beside him,
And the last when she cried for hours.

He looked different than the last one;
He grinned at her as if he knew things.
She wanted to believe he could love her,
But her heart continued to distrust more.

She wished she could just walk to him;
Say "hello" and offer her heart to this one.
She cursed the one she loved in the past;
The past stopped her from love once more.

"The past is over," she reminded herself
But the memories danced in front of her
Sleepless nights that she wasted alone;
Reminding her to never fall in love again.

Gorgeous as he was, she was still scared.
He reminded her of all those past mistakes;
Times when she loved to get pain in return.
Thus, she looked at him and saw future pain.

Another "Hello" that she never dared to say;
Fearful of the past, she let love walk away.
She wondered if she would be strong one day;
Ignore the history and hunt for her soulmate.

29

Sometimes

Sometimes, you don't need a reason to need rest;
Allow yourself to take a well-deserved holiday.

Sometimes, you don't need a reason to be so quiet;
If that is what your soul needs to heal at that time.

Sometimes, you don't need a reason to be angry;
When your heart broke due to no fault of your own.

Sometimes, you don't need a reason to walk out;
If your mind knows why you should not stay now.

Sometimes, you don't need a reason to take action;
After all, you know when it's time to step back a bit.

Sometimes, you don't need a reason to be unhappy;
Maybe your heart has just not found what it needs.

Sometimes, you don't need a reason to be cheerful;

Allow yourself to get rewarded for all your hard work.

Sometimes, you don't need a reason to be cautious;
Especially, when your heart was broken many times.

Sometimes, you don't need a reason for what you do:
Right now, it's okay to pursue what you desire most

30

Looking At Your Eyes

Looking at your eyes, it has never been this real
Every tough road I take, I hope it leads me to you.

Can't explain this feeling: It feels a lot like love;
As if the world has never been this gorgeous to me.

A little bit of pain I have felt, but it's been worth it
Every heartbreak of mine you have cured so easily.

This tired soul of mine has never been able to rest;
Now I look at your smile and think I've found a home.

Ask me to explain: I don't think I can tell you correctly.
Since, seeing you in the crowd, I haven't been the same.

It might be this love that's described in those movies:
I wouldn't know since I have never felt this way before.

You steal a glance every time you think I haven't noticed:

It makes me grin, and I hope you feel the same about me.

I've broken hearts before, but nothing like you did to me:
Yet, here I am once more, waiting for you to realize my love.

31

Beautiful Tomorrow

Tonight the sky feels a little lonely
I lie down on the ground tiredly;
Gaze up at the moon miles away
I wonder what it is thinking about.

More than yesterday, I am drained
Words are stuck in my mouth again.
Million things I wanted to talk about-
One confession I wish I could make.

Away from you, I can't fall asleep.
Your eyes are the only thing I see;
I want to know if you are still awake,
But that one text is difficult to send.

Without any reason, I walked away:
Now, here I am struggling to smile.
I feel a little lonelier than usual
But, no strength to ask you to come.

I told you I wanted to be alone today:
Yet, you are the only thing in my head.
I know that you are also lying awake;
And, you hope I will say "sorry" to you.

Though tonight seems so hard to me,
I know a beautiful tomorrow awaits us.
I know I will fight more for us tomorrow;
Just not today, I am so very exhausted.

I love you; you wish I would confess:
But today, we need to figure things out.
I will think about you under the night sky;
Tomorrow I will come to you and tell you.

32

I Won't Give This Up

For all those days when we are exhausted-
Tired because of all the constant fights.
It's alright if we step back for a while
And realize that we are allowed to rest.

I am aware that sometimes just like me,
At times, you also want to shut down.
So, I promise it's okay if you take a break.
I hope you come back when you are ready.

We have argued for so many years now;
Fighting for a solution to all our issues.
But sometimes a solution is not needed;
Maybe, there was never an issue for us to fix.

I have tried my best not to be too guilty
About the things that aren't in my control.
Live my life how I've always wanted to;

I know that's all you want me to do still.

I know you have tried to listen to me,
Even when you don't see an answer;
To every question that I desperately ask,
Hoping you will have a solution for me.

I can see that both of us are trying hard
To make sure that the other person is happy.
But that doesn't mean we have to pretend
Things are fine when we are crumbling down.

Walking away isn't an option I want anymore.
There's so much I don't want to leave behind;
But when the future becomes a little blurry
Know that it's okay to spend a second alone.

Maybe, that's all we will need to be happy.
Believe again that what we have is enough.
No matter how many things come in-between,
You and I can also stay together for a long time.

33

It's Okay

It's okay if it's not perfect
And that smiles aren't everywhere.
It's okay if I don't feel like waking up
Even though it's late in the afternoon.

It's okay if we talk less;
If we fight more frequently these days;
Or if you feel like not speaking to me
For a reason, you can't even understand.

It's okay to be a little unsure
About every small action that we take;
If I feel you want to walk away from me
Even though you promised to stay forever.

It's okay as long as you are here with me,
Telling me that we have a lot of time still;
If I feel the need to doubt what we have;
Even though I know you aren't lying to me.

It's okay if tomorrow is different
And if you don't need what we have;
If I feel I want to have someone else;
Even though I know, I only need you here.

It's okay if we don't work out still
Knowing that priorities will change.
If you ever feel us drifting further apart,
I hope we can come back to us each time.

It's okay if we ever walk away from this
Trying to find something else to be happy.
Maybe when we come back, we will know
It's okay to hold on to what your heart wants.

34

Fragile

You have been through so much with me for years
Maybe, we have gotten more fragile as time passed.
Now it's easy to ruin what we have with one attack;
I wish we could build our strength back once more.

Not your fault that time has made us weaker lately:
Easier for us to blame when things are not correct.
Hard to trust the moments even when we are happy;
The past looms over anything good in both our lives.

The past is behind us, I know I keep telling you that
But it's hard to believe that when the memories come.
They break you down in pieces and drench you in guilt,
So, you find it difficult to believe my loving words lately.

You and I together, I know you trust we can make it
But some days it's okay if you can't believe that too.
Days when our previous crimes strive to suffocate us
I just hope you remember I am right here beside you.

I might not be able to ease the pain with my words
But know that I know how much things hurt you;
I feel the same but hope time will heal all the injuries.
Maybe in the future, we'll forget the past and move on.

I am at my weakest, so forgive me for not being there
To wipe the tears from your eyes and tell you it's okay.
I know you are trying your best and I am rooting for you
Just like you, I am wishing to make it past this pan soon.

It's hard to see us so fragile, but it won't last forever.
It wasn't your mistake; maybe it wasn't our time then;
It seems impossible now, but I promise we will be okay.
Someday, maybe, things will be just as they used to be.

35

Our Safe Space

Words disappeared from my mind today
I couldn't locate any to interpret you well
I watched you so carefully with a faint smile
I was afraid to realize it might just be a dream.

Every word that we said to each other, then;
Though they were a bit harsh, I was still fine.
Perhaps it was just the magic of that moment-
Everything about us made me the happiest.

I can now fake: we are still in the same room.
Not across the world, which was the reality
I suddenly found out why it felt empty before:
Once your presence eventually completed us.

Too soon to claim we will make it for sure.
But I am willing to risk my all just for you
What we have is what I've wanted for years
Now you've offered it to me on a silver platter.

Just one night doesn't feel enough with you:
We have long ways to go before we are fine.
Scars left on our hearts by our terrible past;
We still have weeks before we can move on.

But this is a good start: I hope you know that.
I wish to see all those pretty sunsets with you;
You don't have to be here for me to adore you;
You don't need to be strong to be with me now.

This space is the only thing we need right now:
An escape for days when reality weighs on you.
Come here when you think we don't want you:
I promise to give you more reasons to love us.

About the Author

Mia is a software developer by profession and a writer by passion. She loves spending her free time near the ocean and believes that music is the best thing in the world. She has plenty of interest in penning tragic tales and poems that tug at the reader's heartstrings. Her work is available on social platforms like WordPress, Wattpad, Instagram, and many more. Mia's goal is to publish writings that make people fall in love with tragic stories once again.

You can connect with me on:
- https://linktr.ee/authormiasanchez31
- https://twitter.com/Weaver_of_tale

www.ingramcontent.com/pod-product-compliance
Lightning Source LLC
LaVergne TN
LVHW041630070526
838199LV00052B/3306